Want to know

nature

Whales

Barbara van Rheenen

Clavis

NEW YORK

This is David. David likes whales. That's why he goes to the beach every day. For hours he stands there, staring at the sea until his eyes burn and his feet hurt. He searches the horizon with his binoculars. What does he see over there in the distance? It looks like an enormous wisp of smoke....

Hurray! It's a whale! A real, gigantic whale!
It jumps out of the water and falls back into
the sea with an enormous splash. As if it's
trying to say: Look, David, here I am!

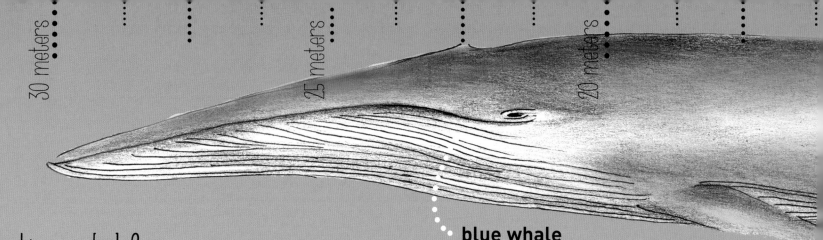

blue whale

sperm whale

What's a whale?

A whale is an animal that lives in the water.
It is not a fish but a mammal, like a human being.
This means that a whale does not lay eggs and that
its young come from the mother's belly and drink milk.
If you compare whales to fish, you can see a lot more
differences. A fish has scales, while a whale has a smooth
skin. A fish can breathe in the water, because it has gills
on the sides of its head. A whale has to come up for air,
because it breaths through the nostrils on its head.

There are over eighty different types of whales.
You find them in all sizes. There are really big ones,
but also very small whales. Those little ones are often
called dolphins. The biggest type of whale is the blue
whale: it can be thirty meters long. It is also the biggest
animal on earth. Most whales live in the sea, but a few
types of dolphins live in rivers.

Did you know
a whale's
nostrils are called
blowholes?

Did you know
a blue whale is about
the same length as three
buses in a row?

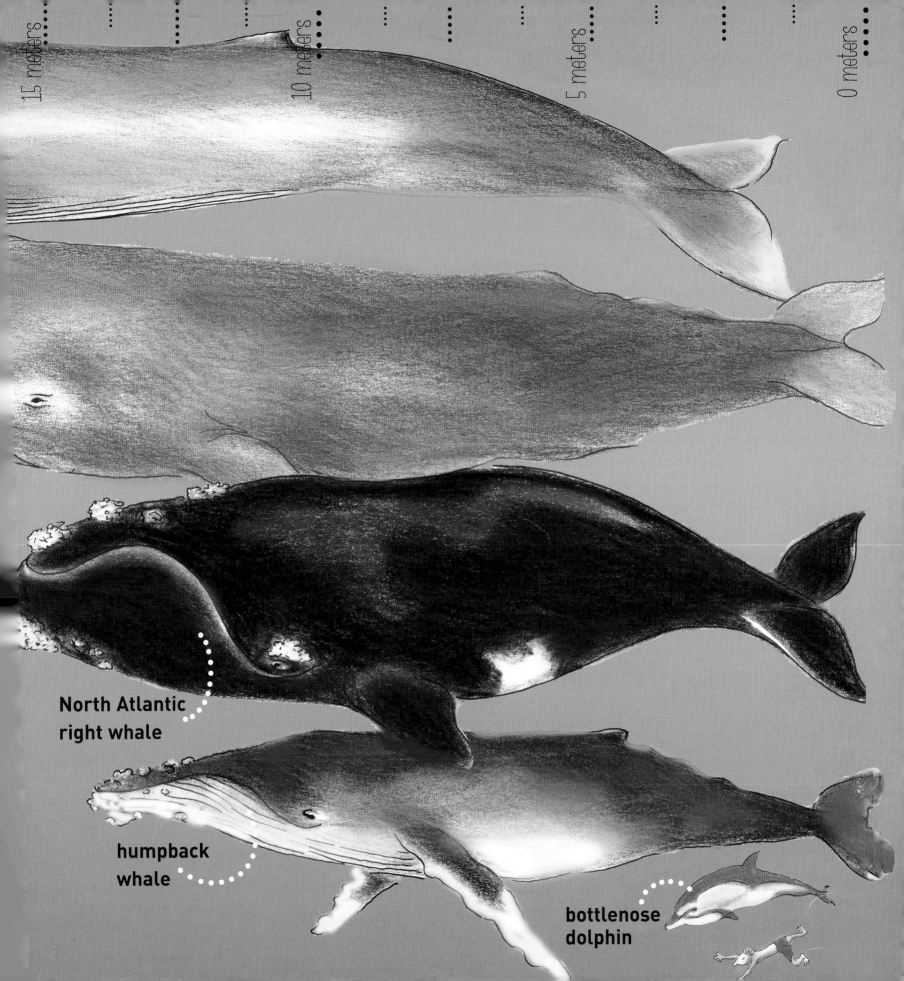

15 meters

10 meters

5 meters

0 meters

North Atlantic right whale

humpback whale

bottlenose dolphin

What does a whale look like?

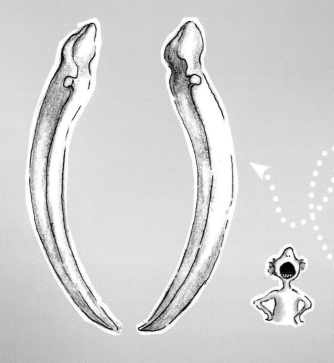

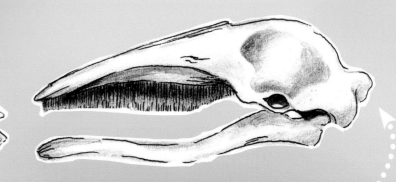

the upper and the lower jaw of a baleen whale

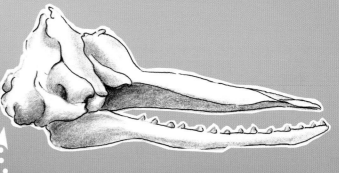

the lower jaw of a toothed whale

There are two groups of whales:
toothed whales and **baleen whales**.
Baleen whales have long, sturdy hairs in their
mouths, which we call baleen. Most baleen
whales have about eight hundred of these
baleen, but some have over a thousand of them!
The blue whale, the humpback whale, the grey
whale and the North Atlantic right whale are
the best-known baleen whales. Toothed
whales don't have baleen in their mouths,
but teeth. Some toothed whales have over two
hundred teeth. The best-known toothed whales
are the sperm whale, the killer whale or orca,
and dolphins.

Did you know
a dolphin can
have about one
hundred teeth?

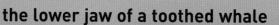

DOG?

WOLF?

COW?

HORSE?

We know a lot about whales, but we hardly know everything. For instance, we don't know for sure what they looked like in the past. Whales already existed a million years ago, but they looked a lot different from the whales today. In those days they probably lived both in the water and on land. They looked like wolves with hooves. The more they stayed in the water, the more their skin became smooth and the more their paws changed into fins. You can still see two little hind legs on whale calves. This is how we know that whales used to have four legs.

Did you know people used to think that whales were dangerous sea monsters?

How do a whale's senses work?

Whales have smooth, hairless skin. To stay warm, they have a thick layer of fat underneath their skin. The skin of whales is very sensitive, so they can feel immediately when they are above water and can breathe. Some whales don't have very smooth skin. The humpback whale, the North Atlantic right whale and the gray whale seem to have big warts on their skin. Those are barnacles and whale lice.

Did you know
the thick layer of fat underneath a whale's skin is called blubber? It protects the animal against the ice-cold water.

Did you know whales do not only
hear very well,
but also sing beautifully?
The males especially
love to sing. This is how
they try to attract
the females.

Whales can see above and under water, but they don't
have very good eyes. A layer of fat on their eyes protects
them against the salt in the sea. Deep under the water
it's so dark that whales can't see a thing. To know where
they are and what their surroundings look like, whales
make loud clicking sounds. The echo of those sounds is
reflected back to them, which tells them where the rocks
or the other whales are. This is called echolocation.
Whales therefore have excellent hearing.

What does a whale eat?

Baleen whales eat fish, plankton and very small crustaceans called krill. They use their baleen as a sieve. They take a big gulp of sea water filled with little animals, then close their mouths and use their tongues to push the water back out through the baleen. All the water goes out, but the little animals are trapped in their mouths. Because whales are so big, they have to eat lots and lots of small animals in order to get enough food.

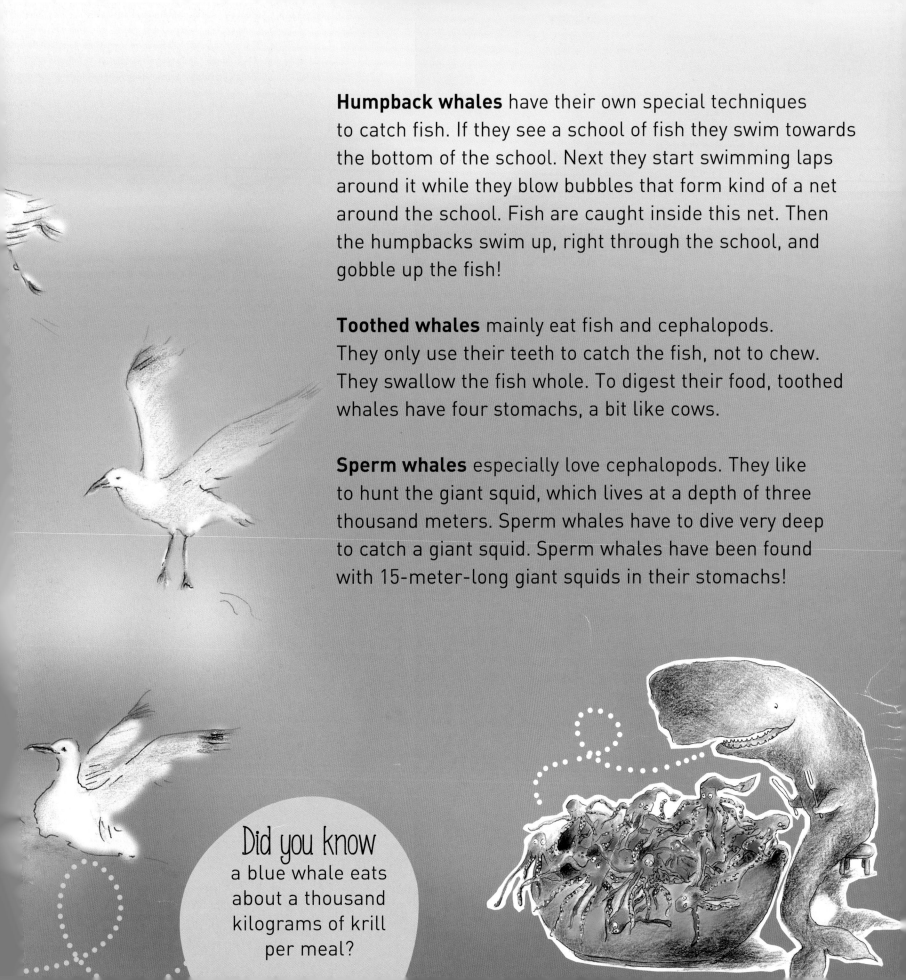

Humpback whales have their own special techniques to catch fish. If they see a school of fish they swim towards the bottom of the school. Next they start swimming laps around it while they blow bubbles that form kind of a net around the school. Fish are caught inside this net. Then the humpbacks swim up, right through the school, and gobble up the fish!

Toothed whales mainly eat fish and cephalopods. They only use their teeth to catch the fish, not to chew. They swallow the fish whole. To digest their food, toothed whales have four stomachs, a bit like cows.

Sperm whales especially love cephalopods. They like to hunt the giant squid, which lives at a depth of three thousand meters. Sperm whales have to dive very deep to catch a giant squid. Sperm whales have been found with 15-meter-long giant squids in their stomachs!

Did you know a blue whale eats about a thousand kilograms of krill per meal?

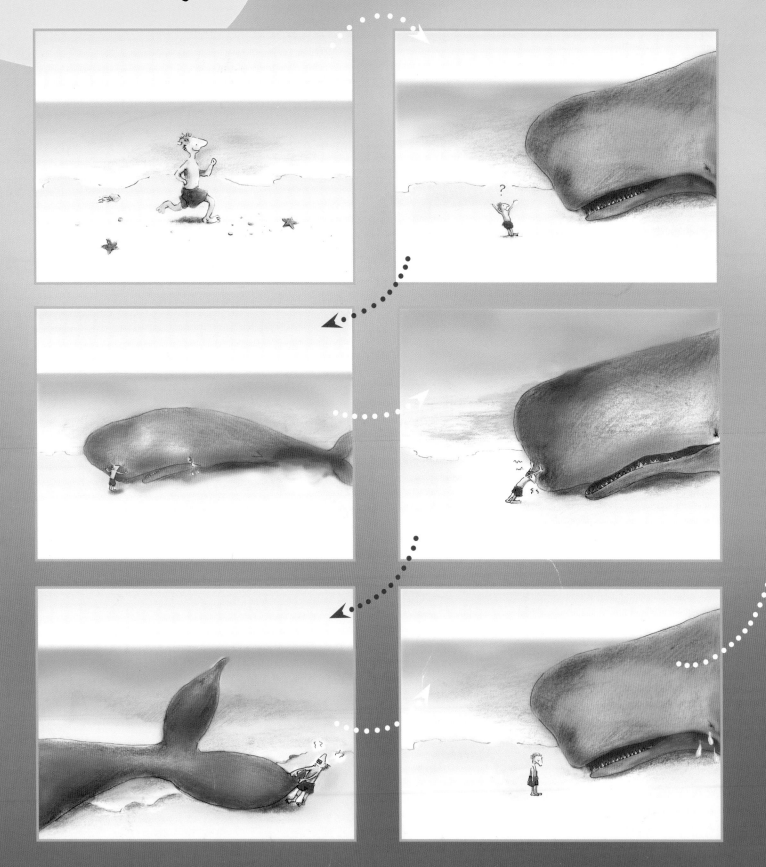

SOS! Whale in danger!

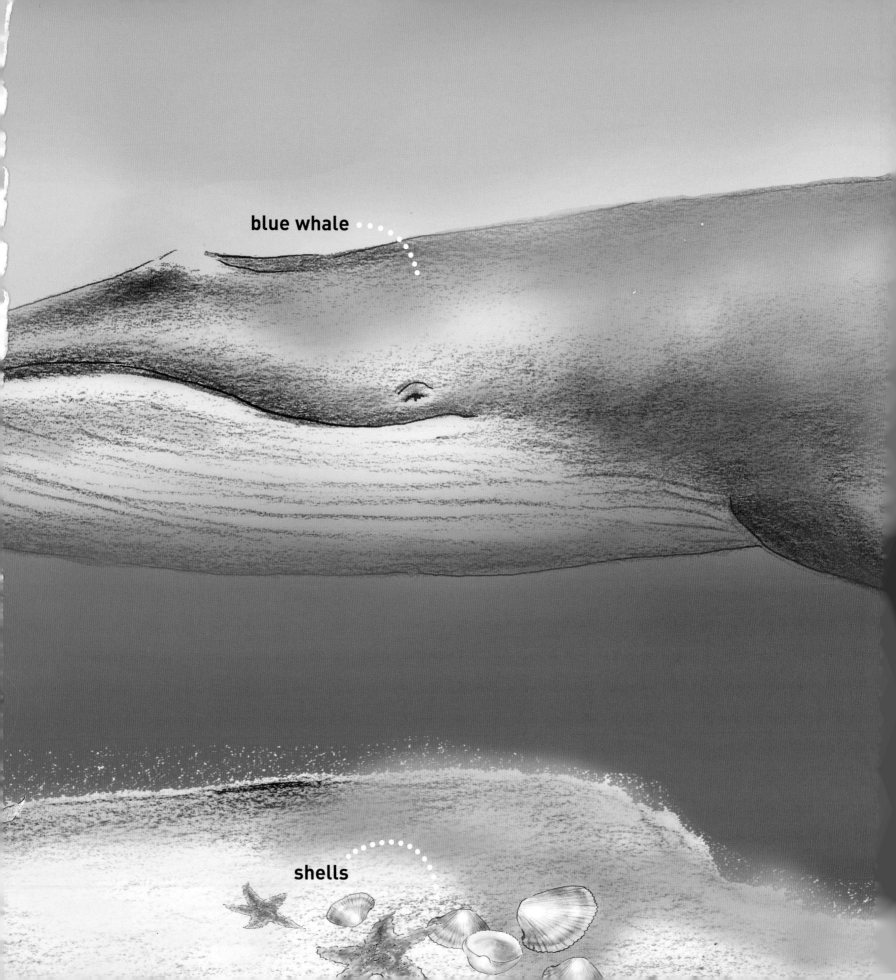

blue whale

shells

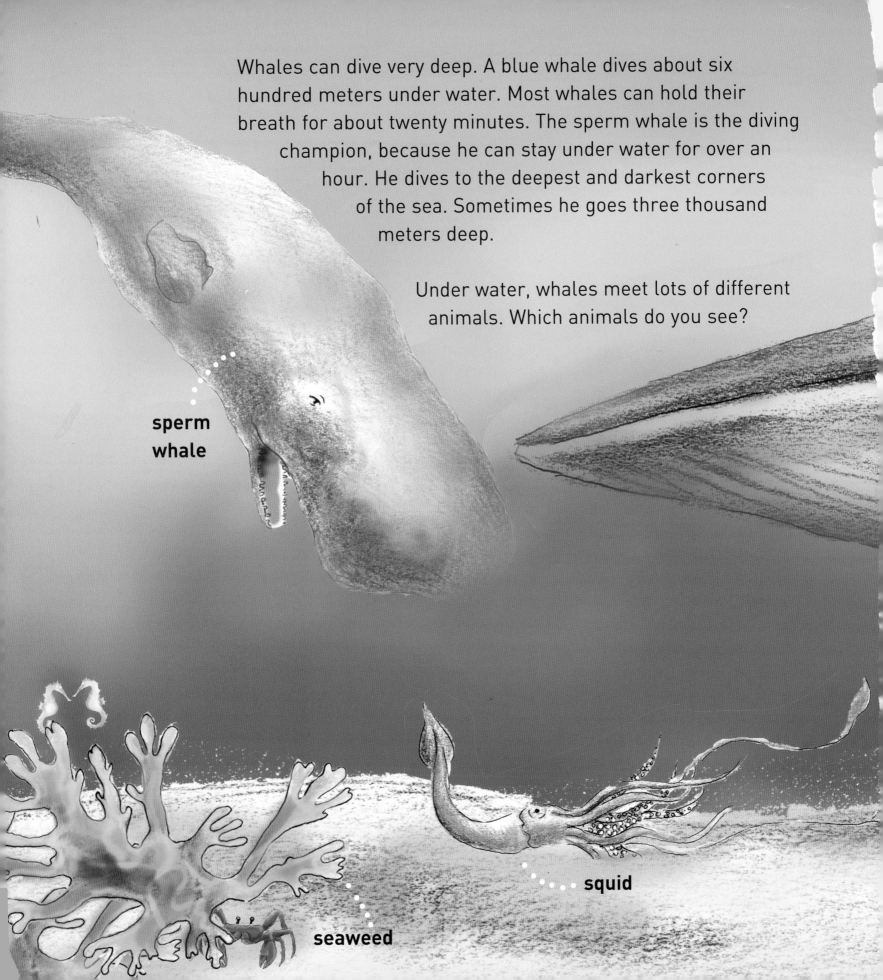

Whales can dive very deep. A blue whale dives about six hundred meters under water. Most whales can hold their breath for about twenty minutes. The sperm whale is the diving champion, because he can stay under water for over an hour. He dives to the deepest and darkest corners of the sea. Sometimes he goes three thousand meters deep.

Under water, whales meet lots of different animals. Which animals do you see?

sperm whale

squid

seaweed

How do you recognize a whale?

Even when a whale does not come all the way out of the water you can recognize it by the way it blows water into the air or surfaces and dives again.

Whales breathe through their **blowholes**, which are in the middle of their heads. If they come up for air, they first breathe out. They do this by spraying out a big cloud of drops of water. This cloud is different for every type of whale. This is how you can recognize the different types of whales.

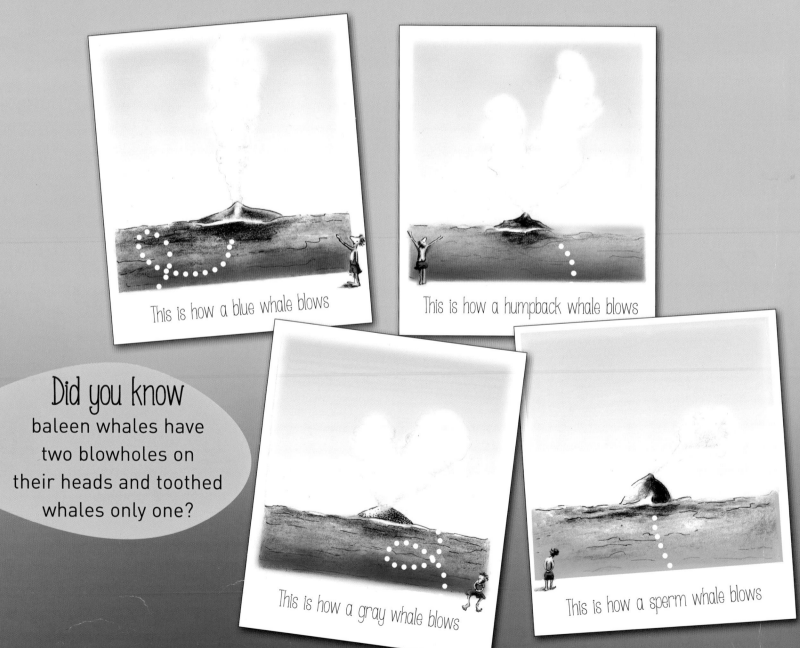

This is how a blue whale blows

This is how a humpback whale blows

This is how a gray whale blows

This is how a sperm whale blows

Did you know baleen whales have two blowholes on their heads and toothed whales only one?

Every whale surfaces differently

This is how a humpback whale surfaces

This is how the blue whale surfaces

This is how the sperm whale surfaces

This is how David surfaces

bottle nose

turtle

crab

Where and how does a whale live?

= mating territory
= food territory

Whales live in all the seas on earth. Some whales stay in the south, others like it better up north and still others travel from one side of the earth to the other. To give birth, whales travel to places where it is warmer. But they find more food in colder places.

Many whales travel in a group. The groups all live separately and don't mingle. Whales love to play. They jump out of the sea and fall back into the water with a big splash. They also hit the water with their tails, so you can hear a big thump under water and at the surface. Humpback whales also like to wave with their flippers above the water. That's how they communicate with one another. For instance, they hit the water to warn of coming storms or danger.

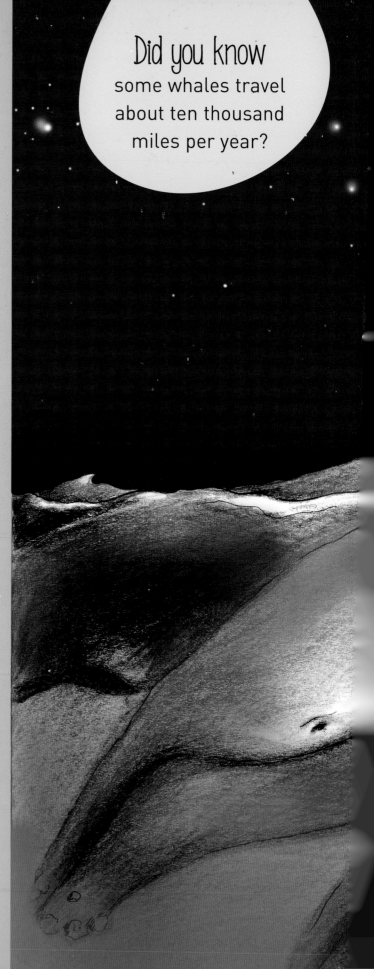

Did you know some whales travel about ten thousand miles per year?

Friends and enemies

Enemies

Whales have a lot of enemies. First of all, there are other animals. Orcas, for instance, sometimes attack other whales. Mostly young ones, but adult whales have also been found with scars from orca teeth. Small animals like lice can be dangerous too. They make the whale's very sick... so sick they can even die. But the whales' worst enemy is mankind. We threaten them in different ways: through pollution, shipping and hunting. The first whale hunters were the Eskimos. Because they hunted with small boats and spears, very few whales were killed. Since then, however, hunting has increased and human beings have invented better weapons, so far more whales are being killed now.

Friends

Luckily, whales also have friends. Different people protect the animals. They try to make sure that they aren't hunted anymore. Others teach people about whales so we can see what nice animals they are. Like David, you can go and watch whales. You can go by boat to an area that's frequented by whales. You can look at them with binoculars. And if you are lucky, the animals sometimes come very close....

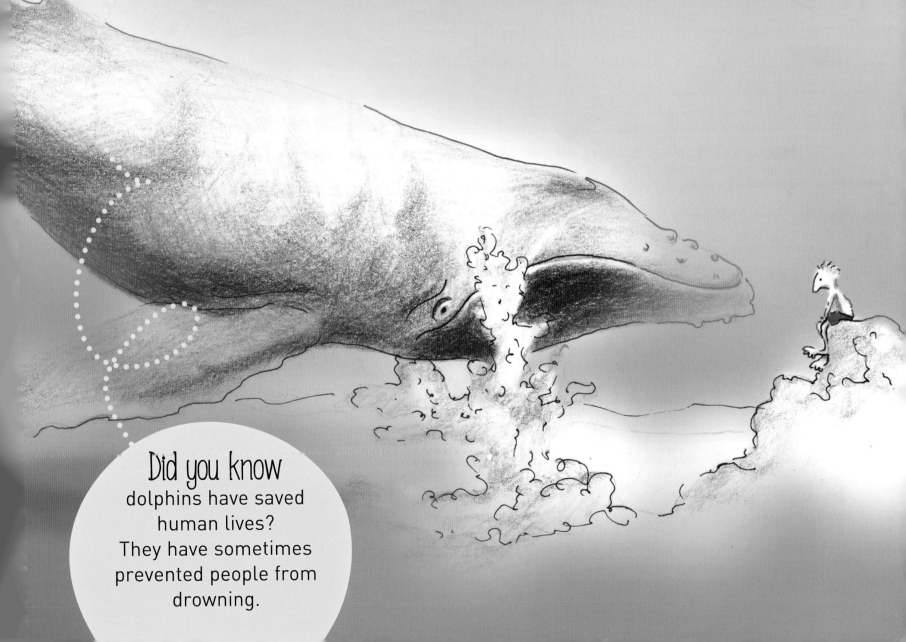

Did you know dolphins have saved human lives? They have sometimes prevented people from drowning.

The song of the whale

I invite you:
Listen to the song of the whale.
Where the moon dances on the waves.
Where the sky kisses the ocean.
Come to this place,
Open all your doors,
Break through your walls,
Listen to the sound of the whale.
He praises
The temple of the sea.
A melody that starts
In the deep blue
And ends
On the fine sand
Of the sacred beach.

Make a paper whale

This is what you need:

A square piece of paper

A pair of scissors

A pencil or a pen

This is what you do:

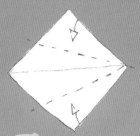 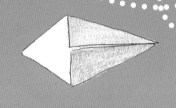

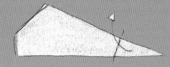 

1. Fold the top and the bottom corners of the paper down towards the middle, so you get the shape of a kite.

4. Fold the tip of the tail up.

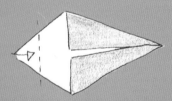 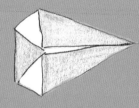

2. Fold the remaining corner to the inside.

5. Make a small snip in the tail and press the two tips open.

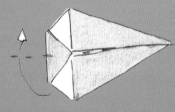 

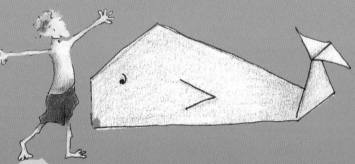

3. Fold the kite in two with the opening facing up.

6. Draw an eye and a fin and your whale is finished!

Miniquiz

1. How many types of whales are there?

2. Which is the biggest whale?

3. Do most whales live alone or in a group?

4. What are the whale's nostrils called?

5. There are two groups of whales. What are they?

6. What is krill?

7. What's the name of the thick layer of fat underneath a whale's skin?

8. What are baleen?

9. Do whales only live in the sea?

10. Which whale is the diving champion?

Answers

1. More than 80.

2. The blue whale.

3. In a group.

4. Blowholes.

5. Baleen whales and toothed whales.

6. Tiny crustaceans.

7. Blubber.

8. Long, sturdy hairs in a whale's mouth.

9. No, some types also live in rivers.

10. The sperm whale.

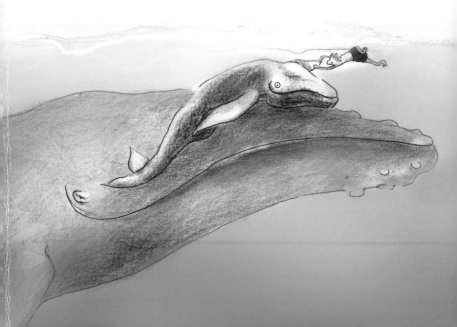

Such beautiful whales!

Do you know which tail belongs to which whale?

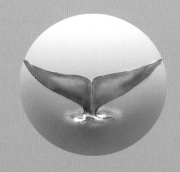

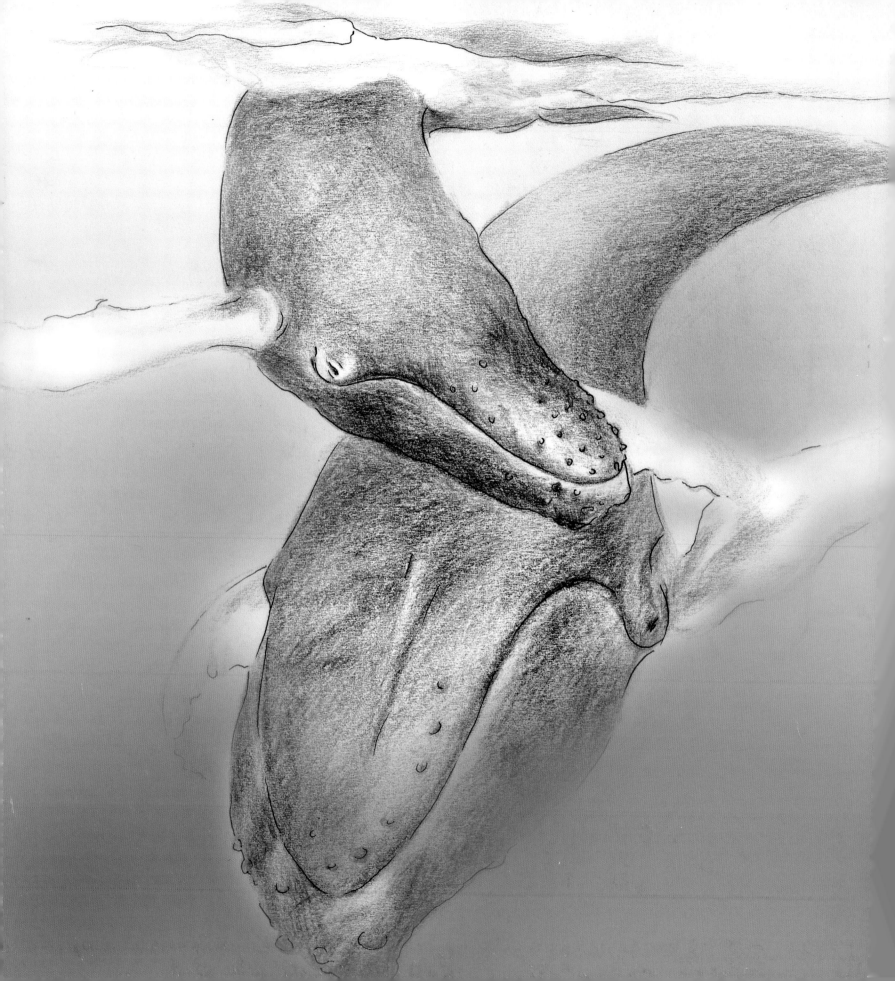